Contents

What a difference!

Amphibians can live on land and in water. A few types of amphibians live entirely in the water and some live only on land.

Not all amphibians look the same. Newts and salamanders have four short legs and a tail. Frogs and toads have two short front legs, two long back legs and no tail.

↓ The African goliath frog is very large. It can grow to 35 centimetres (14 inches) long.

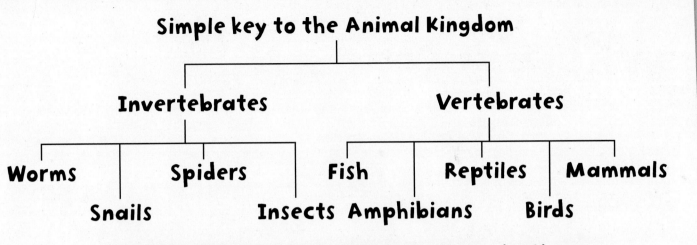

Simple key to the Animal Kingdom

- **Invertebrates**
  - Worms
  - Snails
  - Spiders
  - Insects
- **Vertebrates**
  - Fish
  - Amphibians
  - Reptiles
  - Birds
  - Mammals

Invertebrates are animals that do not have a backbone.
Vertebrates are animals that have a backbone.

AMPHIBIAN CHARACTERISTICS

- Amphibians have large eyes on top of their heads.
- They have four legs.
- They have to keep their skin damp.
- Adult amphibians breathe with lungs.
- Young amphibians (tadpoles) breathe with gills.

The bright colours ➜ of this tiny poison arrow frog warn other animals that it is poisonous.

Where amphibians live

Amphibians must have water to survive. They live mostly near lakes, streams and ponds. Some live in rainforests, where water collects in large leaves and the forest floor is damp and mossy.

⬇ The red-eyed tree frog lives in the trees of tropical rainforests. Like all tree frogs, it has toepads that help it to cling to large, shiny leaves.

AMPHIBIAN HABITATS

- Amphibians that live in cold climates hibernate in winter.

- Spade-foot toads live in burrows in the desert.

- In many countries, where building development has reduced natural areas of wetland, there are more common frogs in garden ponds than in the wild.

↑ The water-holding frog leaves its desert burrow only during the short rainy season.

Some frogs and toads can survive in deserts. They spend most of the year living in underground burrows.

← The fire salamander lives in damp, forested areas, including mountain forests. It spends most of its life on land.

Catching a meal

Amphibians feed on different kinds of prey. Some eat tiny animals, but larger amphibians can eat bigger prey, such as small mammals, lizards and fish.

← This frog is flicking out its long, sticky tongue to catch an insect grub. It catches worms, spiders and slugs in the same way.

← This Australian cane toad is swallowing a small mammal.

Most frogs and toads use their sticky tongues to catch prey on land. When they are tadpoles, living in water, they can eat only algae.

↓ This American bullfrog eats mice, snakes and young alligators as well as fish and insects. Like most frogs, it can draw its eyes back into its head to help it swallow a large meal.

Newts and salamanders feed on land and in water. On land they eat worms and insects. They can wipe the earth off a worm with their feet before swallowing it.

In water, newts and salamanders eat tiny water animals, tadpoles and insects.

↑ The horned toad looks like a dead leaf on the forest floor. It pounces on unsuspecting prey, which includes insects, lizards and mice.

AVOIDING DANGER

- Most amphibians are camouflaged to blend in with their surroundings.
- Many hide during the day and are active only at night.
- Some amphibians have skin that is poisonous to predators.
- Some can puff up their bodies to look larger.

This common newt → is hunting for insects on the floor of a pond.

↑ Salamanders use their tiny teeth to catch worms, which they swallow whole.

Hot and cold

Amphibians are cold-blooded. This means that their body temperature changes with the temperature of the air or water around them.

⬆ The common toad hunts at night when the air is cool and its prey comes out to feed.

← On a hot, sunny day, the common frog returns to the cool water of a pond.

Many amphibians remain hidden during the day to avoid the sun's heat. A few survive in deserts by living underground and near waterholes.

↓ The desert-living spade-foot toad can absorb water through its skin. It comes out of its burrow in the rainy season.

In countries where winters are very cold, amphibians can hide away and sleep to survive the cold. This is called hibernation.

↑ This common frog is hibernating in a hole. It will sleep all through the winter.

HOT AND COLD FACTS

* In cold areas, the tadpoles (young) of American bullfrogs may take up to two years to become adults.

* In warm winters, common frogs may lay their eggs as early as Christmas Day.

* A hibernating frog breathes only through its skin.

A hibernating common frog can live in temperatures as low as -6°C (21°F), which is well below freezing.

When the weather is cold, tadpoles ➔ may take longer to develop into adults.

↓ Frogs living near water sometimes like to warm themselves in the sun.

Getting around

Amphibians move around in various ways. Frogs and toads either hop, leap or crawl, while their tadpoles wriggle through the water.

Amphibians have webbed feet that help them to swim. A few types of amphibians never leave the water.

⬇ Clawed toads spend all their lives in water. They swim using their strong back legs and webbed feet.

This leopard frog → makes a giant leap out of the water.

Newts and salamanders use their four legs to crawl on land. They can also walk along the bottom of a pond.

↓ The alpine newt uses its strong tail to help it swim.

The Costa Rican flying frog can glide up to 45 metres (150 feet) from one tree to another, using its webbed feet as parachutes.

Two types of tree-living frogs can actually glide through the air. They can travel great distances to escape danger.

MOVING ABOUT

- A newt swims using its tail and a wriggling movement of its body.
- Frogs can leap away from danger.
- The common toad migrates a long distance each year to reach the pond where it will breed.
- American bullfrogs can leap up in the air to catch bats.

← This red salamander walks on its four short legs looking for prey.

Amphibian young

Most types of amphibians lay their eggs in pools, streams or damp places such as rainforests and marshes. The eggs will develop into tadpoles.

⬇ These frogs are mating and the female is laying eggs, protected by jelly. The eggs will soon become tadpoles.

Frogs and toads use croaking sounds to attract a mate. Newts and salamanders choose a mate by performing a courtship dance.

↑ This African painted reed frog is calling to attract a mate, using its balloon-like vocal sac.

← Newts return to the water to breed. This pair are performing a courtship dance.

Frogs and toads lay all their eggs in one place. Newts often lay their eggs one at a time and hide each one carefully.

Some amphibians lay their eggs in very unusual places. A few give birth to live young.

These grey tree frogs have made a communal foam nest to protect their eggs. The tadpoles will drop from the nest into a pool below.

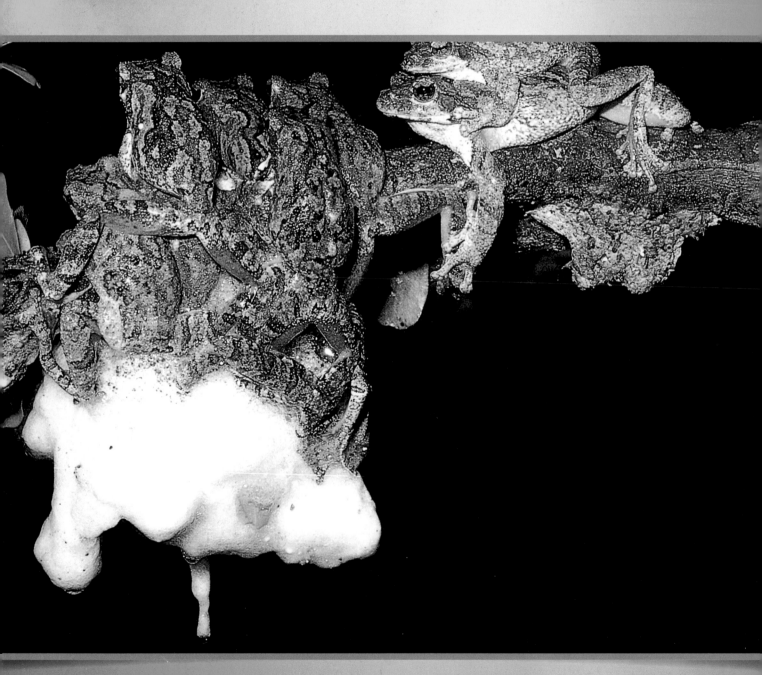

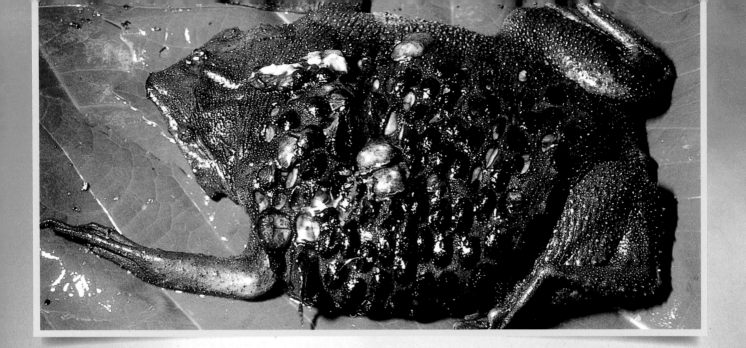

FACTS ABOUT YOUNG AMPHIBIANS

- The eggs of the alpine newt hatch inside the female's body and are born as miniature adults.

- The eggs of the female midwife toad are carried by the male for a month before they hatch.

↑ The female Surinam toad takes great care of her eggs. She carries them on her back.

Life cycle of a frog

1. Eggs

6. Adult frog

2. Tadpole hatches out of egg. Breathes with gills.

3. Loses gills and grows lungs.

4. Grows back legs.

5. Grows front legs and loses tail.

Pet amphibians

Frogs, toads and newts often live in garden ponds. This is usually the best place to see them and watch their tadpoles developing into adults.

↓ This common toad is sheltering in a flowerpot. Many toads and frogs live in gardens, especially if there is water nearby.

CARING FOR PET AMPHIBIANS

* Amphibians are not easy to look after. If you keep them in an aquarium, make sure it has a lid.

* Provide a land area of rocks, soil and branches as well as water.

* Adult amphibians need to eat food that is alive.

* The aquarium should be lit with 'daylight' bulbs.

Most adult amphibians are difficult to look after. However, they are sometimes kept in an aquarium. This must have a land area so that the animals can leave the water.

The larval salamander lives in water, → breathing through its gills. After two months it will be fully developed, with lungs to breathe on land.

↓ This fire-bellied toad is showing its red belly as a warning that it is poisonous.

Unusual amphibians

Many amphibians look quite strange to us. Some of them live in unusual places.

← The caecilian is different from other amphibians. It has no legs and lives in an underground burrow, where it eats worms and insects.

UNUSUAL FACTS

* The Cuban tree frog is the smallest amphibian. It is 12 millimetres (0.5 inches) long.

* The tadpole of the paradoxical frog is four times larger than its parents, growing up to 25 centimetres (10 inches) long.

* If a young great crested newt loses a leg to a predator, it can grow a new leg.

* 1 gram (0.03 ounces) of poison from a poison arrow frog could kill 100,000 people.

* Although the axolotl never develops from the tadpole stage, it produces young.

↑ The Japanese giant salamander grows to 1.5 metres (5 feet) in length. This salamander never leaves the water.

The axolotl is a type of salamander. It has feathery gills like a tadpole and it never develops out of this form. It lives all its life in water.

← The axolotl is like a giant larval newt that never grows up.

Scale of amphibians

Human
hand

Goliath frog

Spade-foot
toad

Red-eyed
tree frog

Water-holding
frog

Fire salamander

Human
hand

Australian
cane toad

American
bullfrog

Horned toad

Common toad

Common frog

Clawed toad

Human
hand

Leopard frog

Red salamander

Costa Rican
flying frog

Grey tree frog

Surinam toad

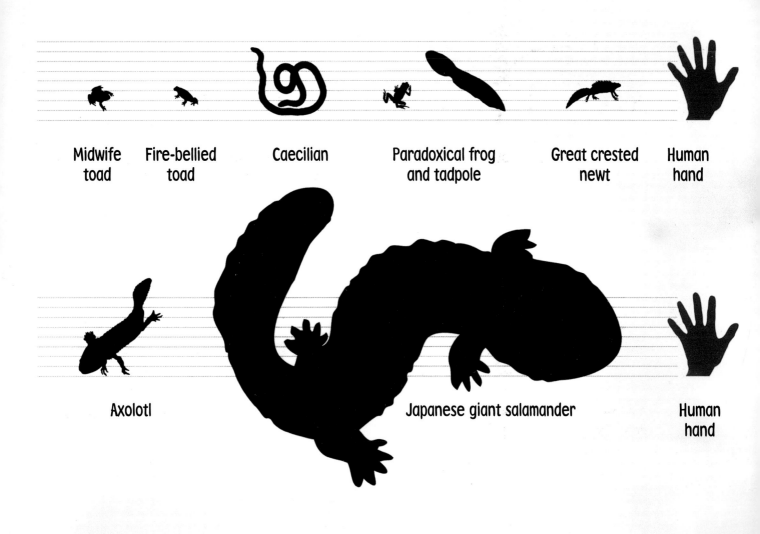

Midwife toad Fire-bellied toad Caecilian Paradoxical frog and tadpole Great crested newt Human hand

Axolotl Japanese giant salamander Human hand

Poison arrow frog Common newt Alpine newt African painted reed frog Cuban tree frog Human fingertip

29

Topic web

SCIENCE
Classification.
Growth and reproduction.
How amphibians adapt to their environment.
Life cycle.
Predators and prey.

MATHS
Measure and compare different amphibians with each other.

ENGLISH
Imagine you are a frog.
Write a story or a poem about your life.

AMPHIBIANS

DANCE/MUSIC
Improvise a dance and create music to represent the movement of different types of amphibians.

GEOGRAPHY
Amphibian habitats - lakes, ponds, rivers, marshes, rainforests, mountains, forests, deserts.

ART/CRAFT
Make a collage or paint a mural showing amphibians in their habitats.

Activities

Science If you live near a pond which is visited by frogs or other amphibians, study the animals and draw a chart to show their development, from spawn to adult. Put in dates to show each stage of development.

English Write a story or poem about a frog. What does it look like? How does it move? What does it eat? Or imagine you are a frog and write a diary about your life, from coming out of the egg, through the different tadpole stages, to the adult frog.

Geography Ponds are very important for amphibians, but many ponds have now disappeared. Draw a simple map of the area where you live. Mark in any streams, lakes or ponds. Find out if any ponds near you have disappeared recently or in the past. If you can, mark these places on your map.

Art/craft Draw or paint a picture of an amphibian. Show either its camouflage design and colours - for example a tree frog or a horned toad, or its warning colours - such as the poison arrow frog or the fire salamander.

Dance/music Through improvisation, show how different amphibians move - swimming, hopping, leaping, wriggling, crawling. Use musical instruments and other objects to make music that represents the way they move. Show desert-living amphibians leaving their burrows when they hear rain. You can make sounds that represent rain, using uncooked rice grains in a sealed cardboard tube.

Maths Use the scale on pages 28-29 to compare the sizes of different amphibians with each other. Compare their sizes with the size of your hand.

Glossary

Algae A type of plant growing in water.

Aquarium A large tank for keeping water animals and plants.

Burrows Holes dug in the ground by animals for shelter.

Camouflage Protection from attack by appearing to be part of the surroundings.

Communal Shared by others.

Courtship dance A dance performed to attract a mate.

Gills Organs for breathing.

Hibernate To spend the winter in an inactive state resembling sleep.

Larval Describing young amphibians between the egg and adult stage. At this stage they are also commonly called tadpoles.

Migrates Moves from one place to another, to find food, to mate or to escape the cold.

Predators Animals that hunt others for food.

Prey Animals that are hunted and killed for food.

Salamander A type of newt that lives more on land than in water.

Tadpoles The larvae (grubs) of amphibians after they have left the eggs. They live in water, breathing through gills, while they develop into adult amphibians.

Vocal sac A pouch that some frogs can fill with air to help them make a variety of sounds.

Finding Out More

Books to read

Grow With Me: Frog by Kate Riggs (Creative Paperbacks, 2013)

Endangered and Extinct: Amphibians by Candice F Ransom (Lerner Classroom, 2014)

Deadly Factbook: Reptiles and Amphibians by Steve Backshall (Orion Childrens, 2014)

Websites

National Geographic Kids
http://kids.nationalgeographic.com/kids/animals/creaturefeature/
Click on Amphibians to learn all about these fascinating creatures and their habitats.

National Wildlife Federation
www.nwf.org/Wildlife/Wildlife-Library.aspx
Discover how your favorite amphibians live!

Index

Page numbers in **bold** refer to photographs.